This is a fictionalised biography describing some of the key moments (so far!) in the career of Cristiano Ronaldo.

Some of the events described in this book are based upon the author's imagination and are probably not entirely accurate representations of what actually happened.

Tales from the Pitch
Cristiano Ronaldo
by Harry Coninx

Published by Raven Books
An imprint of Ransom Publishing Ltd.
Unit 7, Brocklands Farm, West Meon, Hampshire GU32 1JN, UK
www.ransom.co.uk

ISBN   978 180047 361 4
First published in 2023

A CIP catalogue record of this book is available from the British Library.

TALES FROM THE PITCH

CRISTIANO RONALDO

HARRY CONINX

RAVEN

For Amir, SIUUUUUU

CONTENTS

I

BACK WITH A BANG

September 2021, Old Trafford, Manchester, England
Manchester United v Newcastle United

"Number seven … Cristiano Ronaldooooooo!"

Even sitting in the dressing room, Cristiano could hear the voice of the stadium announcer. He grinned at his Portuguese team-mate, Bruno Fernandes.

"Sounds like they're excited to have you back," Bruno laughed. "You'd better live up to the hype."

"You know I will," Cristiano replied.

It had only been a few days since he'd put pen to paper on the deal to bring him back to Manchester United. Cristiano thought back to his conversation a few days ago with Sir Alex Ferguson, the man who'd first brought him to the club in 2003.

"If you're coming back to England, it's got to be United, Ronnie. We can't see you in any other shirt."

Cristiano wouldn't admit it to his new team-mates, but prior to that conversation with Sir Alex, he'd been seriously considering an offer from Man City.

But Sir Alex was his footballing father. He was the man who'd guided him through the start of his career, the man who'd shown faith in Cristiano when he was being doubted on all sides.

He couldn't let him down.

"Must feel weird to be back," the manager, Ole Gunnar Solskjær, said. Cristiano and Ole had played together in the FA Cup final against Millwall, back in 2004. They'd both come so far since then.

"It feels like it was yesterday," Cristiano replied.

"I'm playing you up front today," Ole continued. "We've got a lot of young guys – let them feed off you. Let them do the running for you – they'll create chances."

Cristiano nodded. When he was younger, he'd been full of energy, pace, pressing defenders and charging forward. Now, at the age of 36, he had to be smarter. He had to time his runs to make the most of all his energy.

"I won't need many chances," Cristiano replied. "Just get me one and I'll get the goal."

United were playing Newcastle. The Toon weren't a great team, but Cristiano already knew that there weren't any easy games in the Premier League.

Moments later, he was walking out onto the pitch, barely able to hear himself think over the deafening roar of the Old Trafford crowd. He'd become used to playing without crowds during the coronavirus pandemic, but the noise from the home fans, excited to see him back at Old Trafford, reminded him exactly why he loved football.

They were all here to see him put on a show – and Cristiano was determined that he wasn't going to let them down.

His ex-Real Madrid team-mate, Raphaël Varane,

almost opened the scoring for United with a flicked header from a corner that trickled past the post.

"You'd better not steal my thunder!" Cristiano shouted playfully. He was only half-joking. He wanted to get the opening goal – it was him that the fans had come to see, and he wasn't going to be upstaged.

Soon after Varane's chance, a Man United forward cut inside from the right wing and lined up a shot on his left foot.

Cristiano was instantly moving. Years of scoring goals had honed his instincts and he smelled the opportunity for a goal.

The Newcastle keeper could only palm the shot back into the six-yard box. Timing his run and avoiding the offside trap, Cristiano was there to meet the ball with his right foot and smash it into the net.

GOAL!

"Come on!" he roared, sprinting towards the corner flag as all four corners of the stadium erupted.

He sprinted into his typical celebration at the side of the pitch, leaping into the air and coming down in his most famous stance.

"SIUUUUUUUUUU!" the crowd roared in unison.

"He's back!" Paul Pogba shouted, leaping onto Cristiano's back.

In the second half, Newcastle spoiled the party when Javi Manquillo slotted home on the counter-attack. Cristiano knew that this was his moment to step up and make the difference.

Barely five minutes after Manquillo's goal, United drove forward, with Luke Shaw carrying the ball into midfield. Cristiano was sprinting ahead of him, ready for the pass to be played.

"Luke!" he roared. "Now!"

Cristiano timed his run to perfection, watching the defensive line. Shaw's pass was perfect and Cristiano took one touch, before drilling the ball with his left foot, nutmegging the Newcastle keeper.

GOAL!

He'd done it again and he'd given United the lead again. Once more, he sprinted towards the corner flag and launched himself into his classic celebration.

"SIUUUUUUU!" The rest of the players roared with him as he leaped into the air.

Bruno Fernandes and Jesse Lingard added two more for United, but it was Cristiano who had turned the game and given United the edge.

Some critics had said that, at 36, Cristiano had come back to United to enjoy a relaxing end to a trophy-filled career before retiring.

But he wasn't here for that. He was here for another challenge. He wanted to test himself at the highest level. He wanted to see how far he could take Man Utd. He wanted to get them back challenging for trophies and back at the top of the league.

He wasn't anywhere near done yet.

2
PASS TO ME!

June 1991, Funchal, Madeira, Portugal

"Pass to me! Pass! Come on!" Cristiano screamed, as his friend Ricardo dribbled the ball through the narrow streets of Funchal, towards the makeshift goal set up at the end of the road.

"Ricardo, pass!" Cristiano shouted again, trying to get his friend's attention. But Ricardo hadn't seen him – or if he had, wasn't willing to give him the ball.

He was going to try to score himself. He lined up the shot and drilled it towards the two bundled-up jumpers that made up the goal.

The ball spun past the keeper and bounced along the street behind him.

"GOOOOOAL!" Ricardo yelled. Even the keeper gave him a thumbs up, but Cristiano wasn't happy. He knew he was in a better position than Ricardo and he would've scored too.

Cristiano had already scored five goals this afternoon and another would have given him a double hat-trick. Another two goals and he'd have hit 30 for the week. How could Ricardo not understand that?

He kicked one of the jumpers on the goal posts in frustration, but tried to keep his emotions in check.

But it was too late. Ricardo had spotted him.

"Oh no, here he goes again!" Ricardo called. "Cristiano Cry-Baby's upset again!"

"Shut up!" Cristiano snapped back. He didn't want the nickname to spread.

"You're not actually crying are you, Cristiano?" another friend, Pedro, asked. "He scored, man."

"Yeah, but I was … " Cristiano began, before trailing off. They wouldn't get his reasons. They never had.

"It's only a street game, it's not the World Cup!" Pedro replied. "Relax."

Cristiano ignored him and walked back up the street. His head wasn't in the game any more. There was going to be no double hat-trick for him today.

"Same time tomorrow, Cris?" Ricardo asked.

"Yeah, yeah," he replied.

His heart wasn't in it and he didn't want his friends to see how close he was to tears. The last thing he needed to do was add to his nickname.

He knew from experience that the feeling would go away, and by tomorrow he'd be ready and raring to go once more, desperate to get a touch on the ball again. But for now, all he could think about was that missed opportunity.

Cristiano's mum, brother and sisters were already at home when Cristiano got in. He was the youngest by some distance – his siblings were all teenagers. Cristiano stomped inside and flicked off his shoes in the hallway.

"Hey! They don't go there," his mum, Dolores, shouted, pointing at the shoes.

Cristiano sighed, picked them up and put them in the cupboard.

"Another bad session? How many did you score?" his brother Hugo asked.

"Five. I would have had six, but … "

"Wait, wait, Cristiano," Dolores interrupted. "Before you tell us about your football, you've got chores to do. The match report can wait."

"But … "

Cristiano's mum cut him off with a glare.

"Come on," Hugo whispered, putting a hand on Cristiano's shoulder. "I'll do them for you – you tell me all about it."

He guided Cristiano towards the bedroom, where a mountain of laundry needed folding.

Hugo laughed after Cristiano told him what had happened. "People aren't always going to pass to you, Cris. They want to score too. We need to get you to a proper club, so you can work with real coaches."

"In Madeira?" Cristiano scoffed. "There's no one good enough."

"Well, maybe you won't want to hear what I've got

to say, then," said a deep voice behind Cristiano and Hugo. They spun around to see their dad standing in the doorway.

"Hey, Dad," said Hugo, nudging Cristiano to make him start folding clothes.

"I hope you're not doing Cristiano's chores for him."

"Wait, what were you going to say?" Cristiano asked suddenly, dropping the T-shirt he was folding.

"Well, I know Madeira isn't famous for its football teams, but a friend of mine said that Andorinha were looking for a kit man. I'm taking the job – and I've convinced them to let you join the youth team, Cristiano. That is, if they're good enough for you."

Cristiano's and Hugo's jaws both dropped open.

"Yes! Yes!" Cristiano blurted out. "I didn't mean what I said before. I'll definitely play for them! I need to tell Ricardo. And Pedro. Wait – and Mum!"

Cristiano was so excited that he couldn't contain himself. He babbled on, every thought coming straight out of his mouth. He couldn't believe it. This was the start of his journey.

He was going to be a footballer.

3
FAR FROM HOME

June 1997, Sporting CP Youth Academy, Lisbon, Portugal

"Your coach says you're a Benfica fan," said Sporting Lisbon's youth coordinator, Aurélio Pereira, as he sat down in front of Cristiano.

Cristiano wiped a tear from his cheek, looked up and nodded slowly. "I'm a Sporting fan now," he said.

"Well, Porto beat both of us to the Primeira Liga title this year," Aurélio laughed.

Looking back, Andorinha now seemed to Cristiano like a lifetime ago. He'd been there barely two years, before he'd moved on to Nacional, one of the biggest clubs on the island of Madeira. Cristiano had spent another two years there, developing his skills.

And then the moment had come. Sporting Lisbon.

"So how much do you know about the situation?" Cristiano's coach at Nacional, Rodolfo, had asked him.

"What situation?"

"Ah, OK," Rodolfo said with a smile. "So, this is how it is. We signed a player, I think he's called Franco. It means we owe Sporting about 25,000 euros."

Cristiano shrugged. He didn't know why Rodolfo was telling him any of this stuff. He just wanted to get back out onto the training pitch with a ball at his feet, doing what he did best.

"So Nacional have offered you to Sporting as part of the deal. To make the finances work. You join them, and they start writing off the debts."

"Wait, what?"

"I know, I know," Rodolfo said. "You're a Benfica fan and you don't want to play for their big rivals."

"No, it's not that," Cristiano told him, not quite sure what to say. He wouldn't turn down the opportunity to move to Sporting just because he liked Benfica. That wasn't what was worrying him.

"Would I have to move to Lisbon?" Cristiano asked. He was only 12 years old and he didn't know if he was ready to move away from his family, on the island of Madeira, to live on the Portuguese mainland.

"I guess so," Rodolfo laughed, "but let's not get carried away. You've got to get through a trial first, before they consider accepting you. And you don't even have to accept if they do make you an offer. But I think you should give it a go. I think you're good enough."

Two days later, Cristiano was packing a bag to fly to Lisbon. Sporting were looking at signing a number of Nacional's youth players and Cristiano sat next to his team-mate Albert on the flight.

"Moving to Lisbon, that's such a big step. Wouldn't you be scared?" Cristiano asked him.

"No way," Albert replied. "I want to be a footballer – and we can't do that in Madeira. So we'll have to move to Lisbon or Porto at some point, right?"

"I guess so." Cristiano shrugged as he looked out the plane window. They were high in the sky now, skirting clouds on their way to the mainland.

"Have you thought about who you'd like to play for when you're older?" Albert asked.

"Real Madrid," Cristiano replied instantly.

"Me too! That means we can't let this chance slip," Albert replied firmly.

The trial was set to take place over three days with Sporting's youth coaches.

"Where do you play?" one of them asked Cristiano on the first day.

"Winger," Cristiano replied.

"Not a striker? I heard you score a lot of goals."

"Winger," Cristiano repeated.

Cristiano had quickly established over time that playing as a winger got him more of the ball. He was able to run at defenders, dribble at them, get crosses in and, more importantly, get shots away and get goals.

It was the position where he'd found the most success at Andorinha and where he'd developed at Nacional. This was where he saw his career going.

The trials went well. Cristiano scored several goals in each of the games, including a free-kick from outside the box that curled around the wall into the top-right corner.

He was quicker than the rest of the players, his touch was better and his crosses were inch-perfect. It was the best he'd played in his career, and he was certain that Sporting would offer him a deal.

And now that had come to pass. Now he was sitting in front of the youth coordinator at Sporting, Aurélio Pereira, desperately trying to hold back the tears that had plagued him since he'd accepted the offer to move to Lisbon.

"I see why you're upset," Aurélio told him. "You've not been in Lisbon long. It's a lot to get used to. Look, we'll do everything we can to make you feel at home," he continued. "Anything you need from me, just ask."

"You couldn't fly my family out, could you?" Cristiano said.

Aurélio laughed. "You play for the rest of your career anything like you did in your trial, you can fly them out yourself."

4
SETBACK

September 2000, Sporting CP Youth Academy,
Lisbon, Portugal

"I guess Lisbon isn't so bad, then?" Aurélio Pereira laughed, strolling over to Cristiano as he jogged around the training pitch.

It had been over three years since Cristiano had arrived in the Portuguese capital. The nights he'd spent crying and wishing he was with his family were long gone.

But then the football had started and he'd remembered exactly why he'd been excited to come there. Everything he'd learned and developed at Nacional was done here, but at five times the speed. His team-mates were quicker, they were better passers, better crossers.

Every day, Cristiano could feel himself developing, improving, becoming a better player.

"I guess not." He smiled as he jogged past Aurélio.

"I hear from the lads that you're developing quite the reputation. Something about Arsenal and Barcelona."

Cristiano shook his head. "I haven't heard anything. Anyway, I'm a Real Madrid man."

"When we first met, you were a Benfica fan. What happened to that?" Aurélio teased. "Or Inter Milan? Like the other Ronaldo?" He was referring to the Brazilian Ronaldo, one of the best players in the world, who was a goal machine for Inter Milan.

"Anyway, what are you up to out here?" Aurélio asked, gesturing at the cones scattered around the pitch.

"Training drills," Cristiano answered, wiping his forehead with a towel. "I'm doing sprints to improve my speed."

Aurélio was about to say something else, when one of the medical staff called Cristiano over to the sidelines.

"What's going on?" Cristiano asked.

"We've got the results back from your routine scans. There's something you probably need to see."

"What is it?" Cristiano asked, a little worried and confused.

"'It's your heart rate. It looks like you've got something called racing heart. Its proper name is tachycardia. It causes your heart to beat too fast."

"What does that mean? Is my football career over?" He couldn't believe what he was hearing.

The physio shook his head. "Not necessarily. There's an operation and, if it goes well, there's a good chance you'll be playing football again."

"And if it doesn't?" Cristiano asked.

"Let's not worry about that. You'll need to talk to your mother, get permission for the operation, but we should be able to book you in some time next week."

After Cristiano told his family the news, his mum decided to come to Lisbon. It had been less than a year since Cristiano had convinced her to let him stop his studies to focus on football, but now there was a chance his football career might already be over.

"This could be really bad news, Cristiano," she said. "We need to think about getting you back into school if you can't play football."

"No!" Cristiano said firmly, almost shouting. "I'm not stopping football."

"Don't use that tone with me," Dolores replied, equally firmly. "This is serious, Cristiano. Even if this operation goes well, I don't want you rushing back to play football. You're taking some time off to recover."

"But … " Cristiano began, but a glare from his mum cut him off. He knew better than to argue back.

The operation, a week later, was quick and successful. By the afternoon, Cristiano was already back at home, feeling fitter than ever. Then, after a couple of weeks of rest, enforced by his mum, he was back in training.

"You're even quicker!" one of his team-mates remarked.

Cristiano smiled to himself. Nothing was going to stop him from making it to the top. Not when he'd come this far.

5

PRACTICE MAKES PERFECT

October 2002, Sporting CP Youth Academy,
Lisbon, Portugal

"Go on, tell me again," Cristiano begged. "What was it like, scoring your first goal?"

He was talking to his friend Ricardo Quaresma, someone he had come through the Sporting ranks with, even if Ricardo was a little older than him.

"I've told you already," Ricardo laughed.

"Tell me again," Cristiano insisted.

Since his heart operation, Cristiano had come on in leaps and bounds through the youth ranks of Sporting. In less than a year, he'd moved through the U-16s, U-17s, U-18s and the B team. At the age of just 17, he'd made his first-team debut against Braga, becoming Sporting's youngest ever first-team player.

But, it wasn't enough. There was something missing – his first Sporting goal. He had to know that feeling.

"I just got into the box," Ricardo told him. "And then – I don't know – I just hit it as hard as I could. It went in the top corner. We were already 4-1 up at the time, it didn't really matter."

"Yeah, but it was a goal," Cristiano replied. "The record books will say, 'Ricardo Quaresma – Sporting CP goalscorer'. I want that next to my name."

"It's not that big a deal," Ricardo laughed, amused by Cristiano's passion. "You'll definitely get there."

"I want to get there now," Cristiano sighed.

"That goal wasn't even the best thing about last year," Ricardo continued. "It was winning the title."

Cristiano stared at him enviously. If he'd made his debut at the end of last season, Cristiano would have been given a Primeira Liga winners medal. But the coaches had told him he was too young and that he'd have to wait.

"Pass!" Cristiano said, backing up the pitch. He and Ricardo were running drills. Cristiano wanted to practise his crosses, getting the ball from wide to centre, to allow the attacking forwards to aim for the goal. Cristiano wanted his crosses to be perfect, to get a goal every time.

On the streets of Funchal, he'd wanted the perfect kick, and as he'd learned in school, practice made perfect. He remembered standing at the street's edge, curling the ball towards the makeshift goalposts over and over, a couple of times narrowly missing some windows.

Remembering that pitches were often soaked in bad weather, he had even practised in the rain, until his mother had sternly put a stop to that, after having to wring water out of his socks one time too many.

So he and Ricardo practised over and over, kicking balls until they were both bent double, panting and wiping sweat off their foreheads.

They soon found themselves being approached by Sporting's first-team manager, László Bölöni. He was the man who'd given Cristiano his chance in the first team.

"Cristiano!" he barked. "Can I have a word?"

"See you, then," Cristiano nodded to Ricardo and turned to approach the manager.

"Monday night. Moreirense," he said. "I want you starting. Out on the left. Plenty of dribbling, lots of running.

"And I want to see you doing that thing you do," Bölöni continued. "You know, where you put your leg over the ball."

"A stepover?" Cristiano asked. He'd only learned the skill a year or two before, and it had quickly become his favourite. He loved to do hundreds in a row, bamboozling and confusing defenders.

"Yeah," Bölöni nodded. "That one. Lots of that, lots of tricks."

Bölöni was a man of few words, but Cristiano had taken in the key information.

He was going to be making his first start for the club. His first opportunity to get a goal.

6
SCOUTED

August 2003, Estádio José Alvalade, Lisbon, Portugal
Sporting CP v Manchester United

"Manchester United, huh?" Rui Jorge said, leaning over towards Cristiano in the Sporting dressing room. "I hear they're interested in you."

Cristiano shrugged. He'd heard the same rumours, but thought nothing of it.

"I haven't heard anything," he replied.

"We should be asking you to play badly today. Then

they wouldn't be interested in you," Rui Jorge laughed.

Almost a year had passed since Cristiano had burst onto the scene, scoring a brace against Moreirense, his first senior-level goals. Sporting had failed to defend their title and László Bölöni had been replaced by Fernando Santos, but Cristiano's reputation had still skyrocketed.

He'd talked to the Sporting Director of Barcelona, to Arsène Wenger at Arsenal, and had even heard rumours of Man United's interest. At 18 years of age, Cristiano was quickly becoming the hottest prospect in football.

Sporting's first match of the season in their new stadium was a pre-season friendly against, of all clubs, Man United, and Cristiano knew it was the biggest game of his career so far. If the rumours of United's interest in him were true, this was his chance to prove himself.

"Cristiano knows what he needs to do today," Fernando Santos said, interrupting the players' conversation.

"A hundred stepovers and then cross," Paulo Bento laughed.

"Don't knock it," Rui Jorge replied. "It works every time."

Cristiano laughed along with his teammates. He may

only have been 18, but it felt as if he was a firm part of the first-team squad. He was their equal.

"Serious faces now, lads," Santos interrupted. "This is Man United. We need to be up for this."

He turned to Cristiano. "Cristiano, their right-back John O'Shea isn't very quick, so run at him, use some stepovers and turn him inside out."

"It doesn't matter who the right-back is, that's what I always do," Cristiano said confidently. In the small amount of first-team experience he'd had so far, he hadn't come across a defender who could keep up with him.

"Don't be cocky, Cristiano," Santos said. "This isn't Moreirense or Boavista. This is Manchester United. It won't be easy."

"You haven't played an English team before, Cris," Rui Jorge added. "They're nasty. They'll foul you before they let you past, even in a pre-season friendly. Trust me."

Cristiano shrugged. He was confident that he could handle whatever United threw at him.

From his first touch on the ball, Cristiano could sense that United didn't know much about him. They would back off, giving him space to run into, and he quickly made them pay – driving into the space and cutting inside, spraying a pass into midfield.

A moment later, he got the ball one-on-one with O'Shea and he went into his stepovers, whipping his feet over the ball, before darting off.

Cristiano could see the look on O'Shea's face change. He'd seen that look on defenders before. They were scared, afraid of what he was going to do.

The pressure of the occasion lifted Cristiano's game to another level. His team-mates had warned him about the United players, but Cristiano was finding it easier than playing in the Primeira Liga.

Late in the match, the manager moved Cristiano over to the right wing, showing his ability to play on both sides by tormenting United's left-back.

The only thing missing was a goal. Cristiano went close a couple of times, but couldn't find the elusive finish that would cap his performance.

Nevertheless, it had been the best and most complete performance of his career. If United hadn't been interested in him before the game, they certainly would be now – he was sure of it.

And his team-mates agreed.

"Yeah, so you're definitely going to United, then," Rui Jorge said, shaking his head.

"Why did you do so much?" Rui Bento added. "Are you trying to leave us?"

Cristiano smiled. Sporting may have just beaten United 3-1, but he didn't think he was going to be departing the club anytime soon.

"I'm going to regret starting you, Cris, aren't I?" Fernando Santos said, wandering over. "Somebody wants to speak to you."

Santos nodded to his left, where the Manchester United manager was standing with some of his coaching staff. There was a huge smile on his face. The smile of someone who'd just found their next superstar.

"Cristiano, is it?" Alex Ferguson said, stretching out a hand. "You gave our boys quite the runaround out there."

"Thanks," Cristiano said quietly.

"John O'Shea says he's got a migraine, you made him so dizzy!" Ferguson laughed. "Come with me, let me introduce you to the lads."

"What's going on?" Cristiano asked. It wasn't usual to meet the opposition after a game.

"Oh, didn't they say?" Ferguson asked. "We've been watching you for a while, lad, and that performance has just decided it. There would be a riot on my hands if we didn't sign you – the lads are insistent!"

"You want me to join Man U?"

"If you're up for it, yeah," Ferguson continued. "We've got the fee sorted – we just need you to agree to the paperwork. Assuming you're up for coming to United?"

Cristiano hesitated. He remembered how hard it had been moving from Madeira to Lisbon. But then he thought about the game he'd played today. None of that would have been possible if he'd stayed in Madeira. There was no point standing still in football. You had to keep moving, keep taking risks. That was as true off the pitch as it was on it.

He looked up and grinned cheekily at Sir Alex Ferguson.

"What time's the next flight to Manchester?"

7

SILVERWARE

May 2004, Millennium Stadium, Cardiff, Wales
FA Cup Final, Manchester United v Millwall

"How's England? Are you settling in OK?" Cristiano's mum, Dolores, asked over the phone.

"I've been here for almost a year, Mum," Cristiano groaned. "You don't need to keep asking me if I'm OK."

"I'm just worried about you, Cris. I remember how you felt when you moved to Lisbon."

"This is different. I'm much older now and the club

have done a lot to make me feel at home," Cristiano insisted.

Cristiano had become the most expensive teenager in the world when he'd joined Man United for 12 million pounds in the summer of 2003. The pressure had been on him to deliver, but the United squad had experienced him in action up-close. They knew just how good he was and they'd quickly taken him under their wing.

"Stick with me, Cris. I'll keep you out of trouble, show you the ropes," United's star centre-back Rio Ferdinand had told him.

The United squad was full of superstars like Ruud van Nistelrooy, Roy Keane and Ryan Giggs – players who'd been there and won everything there was on offer.

Cristiano didn't even speak English yet, and it was easy to feel intimidated in the presence of these big names. But he was confident in his ability to deliver and compete alongside them.

It had been that confidence that had already got him so far in his career. Not just his dribbling and his lightning pace, but his determination that he was equal to every challenge. And he wanted to learn all he could from his team-mates.

At first, Sir Alex used Cristiano from the bench – 20 minutes here, 15 minutes there, but gradually he'd forced his way into the team, playing the full 90 in several games and adding a few goals to his CV.

The only thing missing so far was a trophy. Cristiano had missed out on winning the title with Sporting, and it looked as if the same was going to happen at United. They were dumped out of the League Cup and Champions League, and were well off the pace in the title race, behind José Mourinho's Chelsea.

Their last chance to win a trophy was in the FA Cup final.

"Are you nervous about the final?" Dolores asked her son.

"Not about the game. But I'm nervous I won't start. They've got Giggs, Djemba-Djemba, and sometimes Solskjær or Scholes play out wide. The boss might go with experience."

"Well from what you've told me, he likes you, Cristiano. I'm sure you'll get your chance."

A few days before the final, the manager called Cristiano into his office.

"You want to start the game, don't you?" Ferguson asked, getting straight to the point.

"Yes." Cristiano knew it was best to be honest with the boss.

"You haven't played in a cup final before. You're not nervous?" Ferguson asked.

"I'm not scared of any match. I want to play."

"I thought so," Ferguson smiled. "Remember when you joined the club and I gave you the number 7 shirt? Players like George Best, Eric Cantona and David Beckham have worn that shirt for Manchester United. I gave it to you because I thought you could handle it."

Cristiano nodded.

"Prove me right again on Saturday. You're in the team."

Cristiano was speechless.

"You can go now, lad," Ferguson said, cutting into Cristiano's daze. "Don't let me down."

Cristiano barely slept the night before the match. He wasn't nervous or scared, but he was brimming with excitement, desperate to get out on the pitch, desperate to score a cup-final goal.

The Millennium Stadium had a large pitch surrounded by over 70,000 seats, and Cristiano knew there would be acres of space for him out on the wings.

United were up against Millwall in the final, a team from the division below, which only increased Cristiano's confidence that he'd be able to score.

"They're going to be physical, rough," United captain Roy Keane warned him as they came out of the tunnel. "Stay out of any scraps, let me handle it. Just let your feet do the talking. You'll be fine."

Cristiano was out on the right, meaning he would drive out wide and cross with his right foot, rather than cutting inside from the left, as he liked to. But he still knew he was going to make the difference.

He was at the centre of United's early attacks, showing off a few tricks and flicks to test Millwall's defenders.

"Keep it up, Cris. They can't handle you!" Gary Neville shouted.

After about 20 minutes, Cristiano swapped wings

with Ryan Giggs and moved over to his preferred left side.

"I've tired him out for you, now finish him off," Giggs joked as they switched sides.

Right after the switch, Roy Keane found Gary Neville in space on the right wing. Neville dinked a cross into the box and, as the defence hesitated, Cristiano was already steaming in.

He suddenly appeared in front of a Millwall defender, who had no idea he was there. Cristiano met the ball with his head, his momentum giving the ball power, and it flew past the keeper and into the back of the net.

GOAL!

Once more, Cristiano found himself pulling his shirt off and hurling it onto the ground, overcome by the emotion of the occasion. He had earned this. He was going to get his hands on his first trophy, and he wasn't just a bit player – he was the star.

United went 3-0 up after two Ruud van Nistlerooy goals and, after running Millwall ragged for 84 minutes, Cristiano was subbed off. Soon after, he was singing and jumping up and down as Roy Keane lifted the trophy.

"Fantastic! Brilliant game, Cristiano!" Ferguson said, slapping him on the back. "Not sure about the celebration, but love that intensity."

"Thanks, boss."

"The Euros are in Portugal this summer aren't they?" Ferguson said, grabbing Cristiano's arm. "Keep playing like this and I think they'd be crazy not to have you in the team."

8
DESTINY

July 2004, Estádio da Luz, Lisbon, Portugal
European Championships Final, Portugal v Greece

"It sounds like the whole country is out there," Deco said, pulling open the door of the dressing room and listening to the crowd in the stadium.

"No pressure, then," Costinha replied with a dry smile.

Despite what Sir Alex had told him, Cristiano hadn't expected to be included in Portugal's Euro 2004 squad. He'd only made his senior Portugal debut the previous summer, at the age of 18, and there were more experienced players available to Luiz Felipe Scolari, the national team's manager.

But his form for Man United had changed that. Not only was Cristiano in the squad, but he'd forced his way into the starting line-up with a goal and an assist in the group stage.

He'd followed that up with a penalty in the shoot-out win against England and a goal in the semi-final against the Netherlands.

Two months ago, he hadn't won a trophy. Now, after winning the FA Cup, here he was, in the starting line-up for the Euro 2004 final in Portugal. Even for Cristiano, that was difficult to wrap his head around.

Everything seemed so exciting and promising, and Cristiano was looking nowhere but up. But his mum had reminded him to keep his head out of the clouds and his feet on the pitch.

"Don't let it go to your head," she'd told him the previous evening. "Remember who you are. You know I worried about you playing football. You've done so well to get where you are, but don't forget that little boy kicking a ball up and down the streets of Funchal. I certainly haven't!" she laughed.

"Listen up, lads! Only a couple of minutes until kick off," the captain, Luís Figo, shouted. "We know about Greece from the group stage. We were the better team, but they beat us, so we can't afford to be complacent. We're going to have to work hard. We're going to have to fight for this."

Moments later, the players were lining up in the tunnel. "Cris!" Deco said, grabbing Cristiano's arm. "They'll defend well, but we need you to break them down. Just do your thing."

Cristiano nodded without turning around. He was completely focused on performing as well as possible in the biggest match of his career so far.

As Portugal's national anthem blasted around the stadium, it made Cristiano feel proud to be Portuguese. The summer air sizzled as the game kicked off and the Greeks were happy to sit deep and let Portugal have the ball. They frustrated the Portuguese attackers by limiting the space near the Greek goal.

At half-time, the score was still level at 0-0.

"The goal is coming, boys," Scolari insisted. "We don't need to panic, we don't need to take too many risks."

In the second half, Pauleta went close, before Luís Figo had a run that almost led to a goal. But then the match turned on its head. A Greek corner was headed home by Angelos Charisteas and the away side took a shock lead.

The Portuguese fans were stunned into silence, and Cristiano knew he'd have to dig deep to take the game to the Greeks.

Maniche played a pass over the top of Greece's defence, towards Cristiano. He'd timed his run to perfection, watching the line, making sure he was onside.

The ball floated over the top and Cristiano watched it carefully, making sure his touch was precise. It wasn't perfect, but he had control of the ball as he turned into the box. Now it was just him and the keeper. All he needed to do was get the finish right.

He swung with his left foot, looking to fire it into the top corner. But he'd mistimed it and he got the finish all wrong. The ball flew off his foot, up into the air and into the crowd.

Cristiano sunk to the floor, wanting the ground to swallow him up. He'd missed their biggest chance of the match.

"Come on, Cris!" Deco called. "That was brilliant! Let's go again!"

There were 20 minutes left and Cristiano knew he'd get more chances.

He had another one a few minutes later, but this time he blasted his shot over the bar. Then Ricardo Carvalho and Luís Figo went close again.

It wasn't happening for Portugal. As the clock ticked on, Cristiano became more and more desperate and frustrated.

A couple of minutes later, it was all over. The referee blew his whistle and Greece were crowned European Champions, in one of the biggest shocks in football history. Portugal had been beaten in their own back yard, and Cristiano couldn't help feeling that it was his fault, after missing two big chances.

Cristiano knew that the big teams, like Spain and

France, would get chances to win major tournaments again, but Portugal might not, especially on home soil.

He felt the frustration well up in him, turning into anger and upset. Then the tears began to flow. He felt he'd lost the game.

"You're young, Cris. Your time will come again," Ricardo Carvalho said, hugging him. "It wasn't your fault we lost today."

Cristiano sniffed away his tears. Ricardo was right. His time would come again.

And when it did come, he would not miss.

9
HEART-TO-HEART

July 2006, Funchal, Madeira, Portugal

"'A source close to Wayne Rooney says the England star is going to split Ronaldo in two when he gets back to Manchester.' I wouldn't be surprised if … "

"That's enough!" Cristiano snapped, cutting his brother off.

"Sorry," Hugo said, glancing up from his laptop and closing down the sports news site he was reading.

It had been two years since Portugal's crushing defeat to Greece. Still sure it had been his fault, Cristiano had spent those years trying desperately to make up for the loss.

He'd returned to United with a point to prove, looking to get his hands on more silverware after the success of the FA Cup final.

But it hadn't quite gone that way. Chelsea were now the big team in England, and they had swept their way to two consecutive titles.

Man United had also lost to Arsenal in the previous season's FA Cup final. And, this season, Cristiano had scored "just" 12 goals. For him, it wasn't enough.

And then the 2006 World Cup in Germany had arrived. Cristiano had scored his first World Cup goal with a penalty against Iran, and had begun to dream of lifting the biggest, and greatest, international trophy.

But Portugal had drawn England in the quarter-finals, and Cristiano was brought face-to-face with a number of his United team-mates, including Wayne Rooney. In a flash of anger, Rooney had brought his foot down on Portugal defender Ricardo Carvalho.

Cristiano and the Portugal team had surrounded the ref, demanding that Rooney be sent off. It didn't matter that Rooney was a team-mate and friend. Cristiano was going to do what was right.

Rooney was shown the red card and Cristiano had flashed a grin and a wink to the Portugal bench, indicating his joy. He had no idea it had been caught by the cameras.

For the first time in his career, Cristiano felt beaten. He hadn't been making the waves he'd dreamed of when he'd signed for United. He was just another face in the crowd. And now, after this, he was a bad one.

Even though he'd scored the winning penalty in the shootout, the English press were furious about Cristiano's behaviour.

Rumours flew that Cristiano wouldn't be allowed back to Manchester, that he'd be sold, that it was him or Rooney.

So, after Portugal had been knocked out by France in the semis, Cristiano flew home to Portugal, not to Manchester. He didn't know what he was going to do.

"Come on Cris," his brother Hugo said, touching

Cristiano's shoulder gently. "Don't let the press get to you."

"It's not just that," Cristiano muttered, looking up at his brother miserably. "What if my luck has finally run out? What if this is it for my football career?"

"Luck?" Hugo stared at his little brother. "You've worked so hard to get to where you are now, Cris. You may have had a little luck with Dad becoming a kit man, but after that it's all been you. Don't let the tabloids make you forget that."

"I know, but you know the English," Cristiano replied. "They don't forget this kind of thing. They still talk about Maradona's handball, and that was 20 years ago."

"What does Fergie think?" Hugo asked.

"He says it's fine. I even spoke to Rooney, and he said there's no hard feelings. He said he wants me back."

"Do you know, when you were a kid, when were you at your best?" Hugo interrupted, sitting down next to his brother. "When someone said you wouldn't make it, or laughed at you for messing up a trick. When you've got a point to prove. That's when."

Hugo paused, to let it sink in. Then he added, "So

go back to United and show the world that you're no cheat. You're Cristiano Ronaldo."

Cristiano lay on his bed, looking up at the ceiling and thinking about what Hugo had said. His words had helped a little.

Then Hugo's voice drifted up the stairs.

"Cris! It's the phone. For you!"

"Hello?" Cristiano said flatly as he grabbed the phone.

"Cristiano? It's Sven," said a distinctive voice. Sven-Göran Eriksson had just stepped down as manager for England. Cristiano swallowed hard.

"Hi Sven, how are you?" he said.

"I'm OK, thank you. But I'm sure you've been better."

Cristiano said nothing.

"I just wanted to call to remind you of something that I was told as a younger player," Sven said.

Cristiano shuffled and looked down. He was sure Sven was about to yell at him, or call him a cheat.

"Football isn't just about the game on the pitch, Cris. It's about mind games as well. You can't lose to those sorts of things. You have to work around it. That's the life of a professional footballer."

Cristiano nodded, then remembered that Sven couldn't see him. "Oh, yeah, I know. I just … I don't know, I'm just not feeling the support from the club after what happened."

Sven sighed. "When you play football at this level, it's hard. But you have to be harder, have to work harder. Can you do that?"

Cristiano felt the fire in his chest, which had been dulled in the weeks since the incident with Rooney, brighten a little.

"Yeah," he said, "I think I can."

Hugo was there when Cristiano put down the phone.

"You can't leave United because of this, Cris," he said. "You fought hard to get there. You want to have a comeback? Do it Cristiano's way. Work harder, get better. Remind people exactly what got you to United in the first place."

Cristiano knew that Hugo was right. Man United weren't annoyed with him, only the English press.

He stood up and lifted his head up high. He was going to show them all just how good he could be.

10

BOUNCE BACK

April 2007, Old Trafford, Manchester, England
Manchester United v A.S. Roma

"How many are you on?" Rooney asked him, as they stood in the tunnel. "How many do you need?"

"18," Cristiano replied. "I need two more to hit 20."

Cristiano had spent the summer at home in Madeira, spending much-needed time with his family and taking time away from Manchester to refocus.

He had always been skinny and quick, but now he

wanted to get stronger, both physically and mentally. He'd rewritten his workouts to build muscle, slotting exercises into his daily routine so that they became habits.

When he'd met up with his old friends for a friendly game in Funchal, Pedro had whistled when they'd seen him coming up the street.

"Look at you, Cristiano!" he'd exclaimed. "You look great. United aren't even going to recognise you."

It had been a long time since Cristiano had played a game of football like this – not to win a trophy or a title or to break a record, but just for fun.

As he stood amongst his friends again, laughing, taking penalties, he felt again that love he'd had for the beautiful game as a kid. Some of the tension that had built up over the weeks melted away.

When they played, Cristiano could feel the difference in his game. He could keep the ball under pressure, even in the Portuguese heat, and when Pedro had shot the ball towards him, he'd jumped so high for a header that it seemed as if he could have brushed the sun.

Now, months later, back in Manchester, Cristiano was dominating the Premier League, guiding United to the top of the table. He was favourite to win PFA Player of the Year, but United were also still in the Champions League, and Cristiano had his sights set on winning club football's biggest trophy.

Every year since Cristiano had arrived at United, he'd had a bet with Ferguson on how many goals he'd score in the season. In his first season it had been £100 and 10 goals. Cristiano had lost. For the next two seasons it had been 15 – and he'd lost again.

"Cris, Mike Phelan told me you want to raise the bet. £400?" Ferguson grinned.

"Yes," Cristiano replied. "And I want 20 goals. And you're taking it this time if I lose." For the last few years, Ferguson had refused to accept Cristiano's money.

"Son," Ferguson said, looking him in the eyes. "I have a feeling I won't be the one winning money."

But the first leg of United's quarter-final tie against Roma didn't go to plan, when they lost 2-1 in Italy. Man U had never won a Champions League tie after losing the first leg but, instead of feeling deflated, Cristiano knew that if he was in the team, United could turn the tie around. He had done the work, and he was ready.

"Tonight is a better time than any to get your first Champions League goal then! I think you could get those two tonight," Rooney told him.

Cristiano nodded, jumping up and down to warm his muscles up. He'd played 29 matches in the Champions League without scoring. Today he would make sure that number didn't hit 30.

The crowd at Old Trafford were loud and intimidating, unsettling Roma and helping United get off to the perfect start. Cristiano played the ball inside to Michael Carrick, who curled a shot past the keeper from outside the box. Wayne Rooney and Alan Smith soon added to the lead and United were suddenly 4-2 up on aggregate.

Just before half-time, Cristiano got his moment. He found himself in plenty of space, one-on-one with Cristian Chivu. A couple of stepovers, then he drove into the box. He could see Rooney in the corner of his eye, but there was only one thing on his mind.

He blasted the ball hard, towards the near post. It flew low and slammed home into the net.

"GOOOOOOOAL!" Cristiano shouted, as he jogged away to celebrate.

He had done it. He'd got his first Champions League goal.

He turned and sprinted towards Ferguson on the touchline, his team-mates mobbing him as he did.

"One more to twenty," he gasped at Ferguson.

"Go and get it, son," Fergie replied, patting his pocket. "I've got the cash right here."

Five minutes after the half-time break, Cristiano met a Ryan Giggs cross at the back post and he had his twentieth goal of the season.

"SIUUUUUU!" Cristiano shouted, pumping his fist towards the crowd as Alan Smith jumped on his back.

Michael Carrick and Patrice Evra added two more goals to seal a famous 7-1 win and a place in the Champions League semi-finals. But Cristiano didn't even care about that. He had his 20 goals.

As he applauded the home crowd, all the doubts of the summer were washed away by their cheers. He was going to be a title winner. He had proved everyone wrong.

From now on, the only way was up.

II
EUROPEAN GLORY

May 2008, Luzhniki Stadium, Moscow, Russia
Champions League Final, Manchester United v Chelsea

"How many did you score last year?" United coach René Meulensteen asked, as he set up some cones on the training pitch.

"Twenty-three," Cristiano replied proudly.

"So you were PFA Player of the Year, you've got over 50 goals for United and almost 50 Portugal caps – at what, 22?"

Cristiano nodded.

"But you've never ever practised finishing before?" Meulensteen said, shaking his head. "Do you know how good you could be? You could explode. You've got the skills and the technique, but you always go for the spectacular, the top-corner finish."

Cristiano shrugged.

"OK, look what I've done," Meulensteen said, pointing at the cones. "There's different zones in the penalty area," he continued. "If you're in one zone, it's best to drill it, go with a laces shot. In another area, a chip is best. If the ball comes from one direction, you've got to do something different. Sometimes you take one touch, sometimes shoot first time."

"How will I know what to do?" Cristiano asked. There were so many zones and so many different instructions.

"We're going to practise," Meulensteen replied. "Me, you and Mike Phelan. You're going to practise until it's instinct. Until it's all you know."

"Why me? Why not Rooney? Why not everyone?"

"Not everyone can do it, Cris," Meulensteen replied. "You can be the best. I know you can."

Ahead of the new season, Cristiano worked relentlessly with Meulensteen on his shooting. Every time he scored a goal, he would get a nod from the assistant manager. When he hit 25, he got a slight smile. When he hit 30, he got a bigger smile. And when he scored his 40th goal of the season, he got a handshake from the assistant.

By now, Cristiano had accepted that not every goal needed to look spectacular. A goal was a goal, no matter how it found its way into the back of the net.

But tonight was the 2008 Champions League final. It was Cristiano's first Champions League final and, in a twist of fate, it pitted United against their English rivals – Chelsea.

"We know all about these lads," Ferguson told the team before the match. "We know Drogba is strong, we know Lampard is a good finisher, we know Terry's a great defender. But we're the champions of England! We're the better team – and they know it."

"We've got the mental edge. Don't let them forget it!" Rio Ferdinand shouted.

Moments later, Cristiano and the other players were

lining up on the pitch as the Champions League anthem played. The music inspired Cristiano to try to play the best match of his life.

Shortly after kick-off, René Meulensteen called Cristiano over to the sidelines.

"Essien is playing out of position at right-back," he said. "You've got him in the air all day long. Just be ready when the cross comes in."

A few minutes later, Wes Brown lifted a ball into the box. It travelled over Essien, towards the back post, where Cristiano soared into the air. He knew exactly where he wanted to place the ball – down and into the bottom corner, out of the reach of Petr Čech.

And that's exactly where it went. Goal number 42 of the season, his first in a Champions League final and his first against Chelsea, had given United the lead.

"Keep your heads, lads!" Rio Ferdinand shouted, as Cristiano's team-mates mobbed him. "There's a long way to go!"

But Chelsea had pushed United all the way in the Premier League, and they weren't letting this go without a fight. The Blues quickly began to dominate, and went close with a couple of chances, until eventually Frank Lampard equalised just before half-time.

From then on, it was anyone's game. Tevez almost got a goal for United. Lampard hit the cross bar. Half-time became full-time, and full-time became extra-time.

It had been a long season for both teams, and players began to get cramps and injuries in the second half. Didier Drogba was sent off and, although both teams had chances, neither one could find a breakthrough. Penalties loomed.

Cristiano was up third for United. Both teams had scored their first two penalties and the pressure was on him. He placed the ball on the spot, wiped the rain out of his eyes and took a few steps back. He'd scored penalties in shootouts before. He didn't feel nervous.

He stuttered in his run-up and then drove it hard towards his left. He looked on as Čech dived the right way and met the ball with a huge glove, flinging the ball away from the goal. It had been saved. Cristiano may have just cost United the Champions League.

Everyone scored their penalties until it came to Chelsea's captain, John Terry. If he scored, Chelsea were champions. As the rain poured down, Cristiano held his head in his hands and closed his eyes. He couldn't bear to watch.

He heard the cheers a moment later, but instead of coming from the Chelsea fans, it was his United team-mates who were celebrating. Terry had slipped on the wet grass and hit the post, meaning that United were still alive.

Now it was sudden death. It felt as if it was going on for an eternity, until Cristiano watched the huge green figure of United keeper Edwin van der Sar throw himself to his right and block the penalty of Nicolas Anelka.

United were European Champions!

As the rest of Cristiano's team-mates ran off to celebrate with van der Sar, Cristiano collapsed to the ground, lying on his stomach with his head in his hands, tears in his eyes.

The moment he'd dreamed of as a child had finally arrived. And it was even sweeter than he'd ever imagined.

12

MESSI V RONALDO

May 2009, Stadio Olimpico, Rome, Italy
Champions League Final, Barcelona v Manchester United

"You always told me you'd play for Real Madrid one day, Cris," Hugo said. "So why haven't you gone yet?"

The summer after United's Champions League success had been full of rumours, and Cristiano had been at the centre of it all. Officials from Real Madrid had reached out to him personally, willing to bid a world record fee of (it was said) almost 100 million euros to sign him.

"I can't just say yes," Cristiano replied. "United and Ferguson have done so much for me. They've been like family."

To Cristiano, family was everything. With the money he'd earned from playing with United, he'd been able to fund a cancer centre in Madeira, in the hospital that had saved his mum's life when she'd had cancer.

In a way, Cristiano felt that he owed United more than just his career.

"If you don't push these things, then you won't get what you want," Hugo told him.

"I owe everything to United, Hugo. Maybe I'll move to Real Madrid in the future, but I'm just not sure that now is the time."

If he was honest, Cristiano thought that if Real Madrid stayed true to their word and offered 100 million euros, then United wouldn't be able to say no. So it would happen anyway, whether he pushed or not.

But Ferguson made it clear to Cristiano that there was no way he was leaving.

"You're our star player, Cris," Fergie said. "You belong here at United."

But as United sealed their third consecutive Premier League title, Cristiano's mind was elsewhere.

"It's obvious you're distracted, Cris," René Meulensteen said during one of their shooting sessions.

"I'm trying not to be," Cristiano replied. The thought of playing for Real Madrid had been circling round and round in his head since they had approached him. Suddenly Cristiano had felt like a kid again, afraid of making the decision to move to Lisbon, away from his family.

"Do you still want to go to Real?" Meulensteen asked.

"It's been my dream since I was a boy in Madeira. But I'm not sure they'll have me any more," Cristiano admitted. He knew he could trust the coach.

"You won the Ballon d'Or, which, in case you forgot, is given to the best player in the world, and you're still just 24. They'd be mad not to want you," Meulensteen said. "If you don't go, you could become a legend here. But if you leave, you need to leave on a high. Give them something to remember you by."

"You're talking about Saturday," Cristiano sighed.

On Saturday evening, Man United were involved

in their second consecutive Champions League final, looking to become the first club to win two consecutive Champions League trophies.

But it was more than just a Champions League final. It was more even than Fergie's Man Utd against Pep Guardiola's Barcelona. It was the two best players in the world going up against each other – Cristiano Ronaldo against Lionel Messi.

Some people thought that Messi had deserved the Ballon d'Or instead of Cristiano so, with the eyes of the world watching, Cristiano desperately wanted to prove why it was given to him.

Cristiano almost scored twice inside ten minutes, but then the game quickly swung in Barcelona and Messi's favour. Andrés Iniesta threaded the ball into Samuel Eto'o, who cut inside and poked a shot beneath van der Sar at the near post.

United were 1-0 down.

Barcelona were a team who dominated possession, and even though United were a goal down and chasing the game, they struggled to get a foothold. After being so involved at the beginning of the match, Cristiano watched helplessly as Barca ran rings around The Red Devils.

He could only watch and grit his teeth as, in the 70th minute, the ball was lifted into the box, towards the head of Lionel Messi, who rose in the air and looped a header over the keeper.

United were 2-0 down and, even worse, Messi had scored.

There wasn't a way back for United and the referee soon blew the final whistle.

United had lost.

Cristiano looked up at the sky, blinking away the tears of frustration that filled his eyes. This wasn't the way he wanted to end his Man United career.

But now his mind was made up. He was going to Real Madrid. He was going to go toe-to-toe with Messi and Barcelona.

And he was going to win.

13
EL CLÁSICO

May 2009, Stadio Olimpico, Rome, Italy
Champions League Final, Barcelona v Manchester United

"A world-record 80 million transfer fee, a one billion euro buy-out clause, 80,000 fans just at your presentation … and you think you've had a bad season?" Hugo stared open-mouthed at Cristiano as he rattled off the statistics.

He was right. Real Madrid had wanted him – and desperately. They'd returned to United with a mammoth offer – a world record fee of £80 million.

He'd been presented to a record crowd at Real Madrid's Santiago Bernabéu Stadium. Despite the fact that Real Madrid had also signed Kaká, Xabi Alonso and Karim Benzema, Cristiano was the star signing.

And when he'd scored in his first four games in La Liga, it had seemed to everyone that Cristiano was going to be just as dominant in Spain as he had been in England.

But then it had happened. During the final ten minutes of a game against Tenerife, his ankle had given and, just like that, he was out for five weeks.

It had set the tone for the rest of his season. He would score goals, but then he'd be suspended or injured.

Real Madrid had been knocked out of the Champions League by Lyon and humiliated in the Copa del Rey by Alcorcón, a team who didn't even play in Spain's top division.

But at least Real were still neck-and-neck with Barcelona in the title race.

"Well, Cris? What are you thinking about?" Hugo asked him. Cristiano realised he still hadn't answered his brother's question.

"Saturday," he replied.

He didn't need to say any more. Saturday was Real Madrid v Barcelona, El Clásico. The biggest game of the season.

The two rivals were level on points, but Barcelona were ahead, having beaten Madrid 1-0 at the Camp Nou earlier in the season. So Real had to win this to go above their rivals in the table. Real were unbeaten at home in the league, but Cristiano had lost his last two meetings with Barcelona and he was determined not to lose three.

"It's more than just Messi v Ronaldo you know," Hugo said. "There's a lot else at stake."

"I know that," Cristiano snapped, "but if I play better than him, we'll win."

Hugo knew better than to argue with his brother.

On the day, 80,000 fans were packed into the Santiago Bernabéu, all in high spirits. They knew how important the match was for Real Madrid.

But the game started the same way as last season's Champions League final, with Barcelona dominating possession. Their passing was so quick and precise that Cristiano and his Real team-mates were chasing shadows.

When Real were able to get the ball, Cristiano found himself surrounded by three or four Barcelona players. Meanwhile, Messi seemed to find himself with acres of space on the ball, gliding through the Real Madrid back line.

A Barcelona goal seemed inevitable.

"Close him down!" Cristiano shouted to the Madrid defenders.

It came a moment later. Messi exchanged passes with Xavi, bringing the ball down on his chest and smashing it past Casillas.

It only took a few minutes in the second half for Barcelona to double their lead.

There was nothing else Cristiano could do. Barcelona had won the match in Real's back yard, and the title was now theirs to lose.

The next day, the headlines read, "Messi 3-0 Ronaldo." Although Cristiano had now lost all three matches he'd played against Messi and Barcelona, he wasn't going to let the headlines get in his way.

He might have lost the first battle for La Liga, but he was determined that he was going to win the war.

14
AT LAST

April 2011, Mestalla Stadium, Valencia, Spain
Copa del Rey Final, Real Madrid v Barcelona

"You're getting the number 7 shirt, now that Raul has retired then?" Hugo asked Cristiano.

"Yep. Now I finally feel like myself!"

Taking Raul's number 7 shirt and passing his number 9 shirt on to Karim Benzema wasn't the only change at Real Madrid over the previous summer.

Legendary manager José Mourinho had taken over

at the club, after leading Inter Milan to win the treble.

It didn't take him long to overhaul the squad. Ángel Di María, Sami Khedira, Mesut Özil, Ricardo Carvalho and Pedro León all arrived to help the club do one thing.

"We're ending Barca's dominance," José announced in his first meeting with the squad. "I beat them with Inter in the Champions League last season. I know how to beat Pep. I know how to beat Barca."

José's attitude reminded Cristiano of his own approach. Mourinho was a winner, and Cristiano knew he'd continue doing that for Real Madrid. He was sick and tired of losing to Lionel Messi and the rest of Barcelona. Now, with José, that would change.

Later that day, Mourinho called Cristiano into his office.

"You're the best player in the world, you know that," he said. "They know it out in Barcelona too. They're scared of you. You can explode this year. Trust me."

Cristiano believed in the new manager. He was a fellow Portuguese, and he'd watched Mourinho win the Champions League with Porto, dominate England with

Chelsea, and finally get a treble with Inter Milan. Now, they were in the same team.

It didn't take long for Cristiano to hit the ground running, with braces against Deportivo and Málaga, four goals against Racing Santander and a hat-trick against Athletic Bilbao. He felt stronger, more experienced, and ready for his best season yet.

But then, in their first meeting with Barcelona, they were hammered 5-0.

It wasn't the start José had promised.

Although Real Madrid were second in the La Liga title race, they kept winning in the Champions League and Copa del Rey. This finally set up the ultimate clash between the two sides in April, where they were set to play each other four times inside a few weeks. Twice in the Champions League semi-finals, once in La Liga and once more in the Copa del Rey final.

"If we win all four, then we could win the treble!" Mesut Özil said.

"We're too far back in the league," Karim Benzema reminded him. "But I'd settle for just winning one, just to stop them getting their hands on all the trophies."

"We need to win the final," Cristiano said bluntly. "I don't care about anything else. We're winning that final."

The first match was in the league and, despite a red card for centre-back Raúl Albiol, Real were able to hold Barcelona to a 1-1 draw. Both goals were penalties scored by Messi and Cristiano.

Just four days later, both teams turned their attention to the Copa del Rey final. A packed crowd gathered in Valencia's Mestalla stadium for the match. Trying something different to beat Barca, Mourinho chose a more defensive line-up than usual, playing centre-back Pepe in midfield.

"Let everyone else do the defensive work, Cris," José told him. "Just find space and finish chances. You've been doing it all season, so don't stop doing it now."

Cristiano nodded. With 41 goals in all competitions so far, he was having one of the best seasons of his life.

The game was hard-fought and fast-paced, with both sides flying into challenges and surrounding the referee at every chance.

The referee was doing his best to control it, but

tempers were flying and both sets of players had been completely overtaken by the atmosphere.

Both teams had chances, but the score was still 0-0 after 90 minutes and the game went to extra time. There were more yellow cards than goalscoring chances and the match seemed destined for penalties.

Then, midway through extra time, Ángel Di María picked up the ball on the left wing and fired a cross into the box. Cristiano was waiting in the middle. He leapt into the air above his defender and met the ball with a thunderous header.

GOAL!

Cristiano wheeled away and knee-slid in front of the fans. This was easily the biggest goal of his Real Madrid career so far.

"Yes, Cris!" Álvaro Arbeloa shouted from behind him. The rest of Cristiano's team-mates joined him to celebrate, but he brushed everyone away and told them to stay calm.

"It's not over yet, boys! Let's defend with everything we have!" he shouted, as the team jogged back towards the half-way line.

Real just needed to hold on to their lead for ten more minutes. Cristiano didn't care about attacking any more. He did more defensive work in those ten minutes than he'd done all season, tracking back, blocking crosses, making tackles.

And when he did get the ball, he would drive forward, winning free kicks for his team.

And it soon paid off. As the referee blew the final whistle, it made one of Cristiano's dreams a reality. He'd scored the winner against Barcelona and he had helped Real Madrid win the Copa del Rey.

"Now you've got one back in the score with Messi. 4-1 now, isn't it?" Karim Benzema asked Cristiano, as they paraded around the stadium, posing for photos with the trophy.

"Yep. And we'll beat them on the way to our next trophy too," Cristiano replied with a grin.

15
BACK ON TOP

May 2012, San Mamés, Bilbao, Spain
Athletic Bilbao v Real Madrid

"One game," José Mourinho said, sizing up the players. "One game is all we need. We've not lost for 18 games. We've scored six at Sevilla, four at Atlético and beaten Barcelona at the Nou Camp. All we need now is one win."

A year had passed since Real had lifted the Copa del Rey, defeating Barcelona 1-0. Since then, they'd met

Barcelona eight times in four different competitions. Barcelona had won the Super Cup, they'd knocked Real out of the Copa del Rey this year and out of the Champions League last year.

But Real Madrid had taken the wins in La Liga. Now they were seven points clear with just three games left to play. If they won today, away at Athletic Bilbao, they would be champions.

For Cristiano, it would be the fourth league title of his career and his first in Spain. At last, he would really feel that his career in Madrid had taken off.

"They said we were the boring team, that Barcelona were the exciting ones, but we've been the team scoring goals," José told them.

The club hadn't won the league title since 2008, and there was a huge sense of anticipation and excitement within the squad. It was a big day for most of them.

Mesut Özil and Xabi Alonso were pursuing their first ever league titles, whilst Iker Casillas was going after his fifth at the same ground where he had made his debut 13 years previously.

For José Mourinho, he was after his seventh title in

four different countries, and for Real Madrid it would be their 32nd. There was so much at stake.

"How many more goals are you going to add today then?" Xabi Alonso asked, placing a hand on Cristiano's shoulder.

"However many it takes for us to win," Cristiano replied, lacing up his boots. He smiled to himself as he remembered the days at Man United when his target for the season had been 20 goals.

This season, Cristiano had scored 57 goals in all competitions, in just 52 games. They were numbers that Cristiano had only matched on the streets of Funchal when he was younger, but now he was doing it at football's highest level.

Within 12 minutes, Real Madrid had their first opportunity to silence the noisy Bilbao crowd. From a corner, the ball deflected off the hand of Bilbao defender Javi Martínez, and the referee instantly pointed to the penalty spot.

Only one man was ever going to take it. Cristiano stood over the ball, breathing slowly and waiting for the referee to blow his whistle. The Bilbao crowd were jeering and booing, desperate to see Cristiano slip up. He sprinted forward, before cheekily chipping the ball down the middle.

But Cristiano had completely mistimed it and the keeper was able to flick the ball over the crossbar. As the home fans cheered, Cristiano kicked the air, furious and embarrassed at having wasted such an important opportunity.

"Don't worry, Cris," Sergio Ramos said. "You'll get another chance."

A few minutes later, Gonzalo Higuaín blasted a shot into the right-hand corner to open the scoring and silence the fans who'd been booing Cristiano.

Not long after that, Cristiano produced a brilliant cross that was turned in by Mesut Özil.

"That was all you, mate," Özil said to Cristiano as they celebrated.

Real Madrid were 2-0 up and cruising. Now, they could have some fun.

Cristiano started to pull out the tricks and the flicks that he'd been holding in reserve.

He'd been so focused on scoring goals and becoming

the best finisher in the world, he'd almost forgotten about how much fun football could be. Now he could enjoy it again.

But he still wanted that goal.

In the second half, Xabi Alonso floated a corner towards the edge of the six-yard line and Cristiano attacked the ball, powering it towards the corner of the net. GOAL!

With their arms around each other's shoulders, Cristiano jogged away with Pepe in front of the silenced home fans.

"Thirty two league titles!" Xabi Alonso cried after the final whistle, as he grabbed Cristiano and dragged him towards the Real Madrid fans.

"And your first league title, mate. Congrats!" Cristiano said, putting his arm around Xabi.

"Let's get the boss!" Ramos shouted.

They all surrounded Mourinho and threw him into the air, catching him again on the way down. He was the man who'd returned the league title to Madrid, the man who had knocked Barcelona off their perch.

Now they just needed to do it all over again.

16
LA DECIMA

May 2014, Estádio da Luz, Lisbon, Portugal
Champions League Final, Real Madrid v Atlético Madrid

"So José's gone. And your transfer record as well, Cris," Sergio Ramos said, scrolling through his phone.

"Who cares about the transfer record?" Cristiano replied. "What matters is what happens on the pitch."

The season after Real Madrid's La Liga win had been difficult. Even though Pep Guardiola had left Barcelona, Barca had still managed to beat Real to the league title. Real also lost in the Champions League semi-finals to Borussia Dortmund and in the Copa del Rey final to Atlético Madrid, their biggest rivals after Barcelona.

"It's a shame about José," Karim Benzema said. "Winning that title was incredible."

"He was becoming difficult," Ramos replied. "Dropping Iker ... "

"Let's just see if the new man can top what José did," Cristiano interrupted.

The new man was Carlo Ancelotti. Just like José, he'd won titles in England and Italy, including the Champions League with AC Milan. He had real pedigree.

"As long as we win La Decima, I don't care who the boss is," Ramos said.

La Decima was the thing that everyone at Real Madrid had been craving for such a long time. Real currently had nine European Cup titles to their name, more than any other club in Europe. But they wanted the tenth. They wanted La Decima.

"What about the big signing?" Benzema asked. "Could he make the difference?"

Ancelotti wasn't the only new face at Real Madrid. The club had broken Cristiano's transfer record when they'd signed Gareth Bale from Tottenham for 90 million pounds.

"Who knows," Ramos said. "But with Bale, Benzema and Cristiano, we've got the best front three in the world. We'll call you 'the BBC'."

Cristiano laughed. He wasn't too bothered about Bale taking his transfer record. It had only been a matter of time before the record would fall, and he was glad that it was someone coming to his club who broke it.

"Hey Gareth, I'm glad my transfer record went to a team-mate!" Cristiano had told him in their first conversation at the training ground.

"Thanks, Cris. Hopefully I don't feel more pressure because of it, though. It's a lot to deal with," Bale had replied.

"Don't worry about what everyone else thinks. Just focus on playing your best football. Then you'll live up to the transfer fee without even thinking about it," Cristiano had told him.

Just like everyone else at Real Madrid, Cristiano

was obsessed with La Decima. He hadn't won the Champions League since 2008. In that time, Barcelona – and Messi – had won it twice.

If Cristiano was going to become one of the best players of all time, he needed to win multiple Champions Leagues.

José had reached the Champions League semi-finals three times with Real Madrid, but after beating Dortmund in the quarter-finals and Bayern Munich in the semi-finals, Ancelotti managed to reach the final in his very first season with the club.

By the time May rolled around, La Decima had become more than an obsession. It was the only thing that could rescue Real Madrid's season.

"Third in the league and winning the Copa del Rey isn't so bad, is it?" Hugo asked Cristiano hesitantly.

"It's terrible," Cristiano replied. "Atlético beat us to the title and I was injured for the Copa del Rey final."

"So you think winning the Champions League is going to make up for all that?" Hugo asked.

"I can win it with two different clubs, score in two different finals," Cristiano said. "These are big things.

At the end of my career, these are the games that people will remember."

Hugo nodded. "Well, I'll be in the front row, brother. Let's do this."

The final almost seemed like fate for Cristiano. It was in Lisbon, the city he'd left Madeira for, all those years ago. The last final he'd played in the stadium had been against Greece, in Euro 2004. After losing that, Cristiano had told himself that he'd never lose a final in Lisbon again.

Real were up against Atlético, turning the Champions League final into a Madrid derby. Cristiano wanted revenge for their beating his team to the La Liga and Copa del Rey titles last season.

"This is it then, boys!" the captain, Iker Casillas, shouted in the dressing room before kick-off. "Atlético beat us to two big titles last season, but they're not going to do it a third time."

Despite the captain's encouragement, the game got off to the worst possible start when Diego Godín's header looped over the line, despite the best efforts of Iker Casillas. Atlético had the lead.

For the next hour, Real Madrid wasted chance after chance. As the game entered the 90th minute, it looked as if Atlético were going to be crowned champions.

But in the third minute of added time, Real Madrid won a corner. It was their last chance to score. Luka Modric´ floated the ball in and Cristiano leapt into the air. The ball travelled over him, but only as far as Sergio Ramos. The Spanish defender directed a header past the dive of Thibaut Courtois – and Real were level!

The full-time whistle blew, and the Atlético players and fans couldn't believe what had just happened. With 30 minutes of extra time to play, Real Madrid now had the wind in their sails.

Ten minutes before the end of the 120 minutes, a shot from Ángel Di María was blocked by Courtois, but only as far as Gareth Bale, who managed to head the rebound into the empty net.

"Told you he'd make the difference!" Benzema said to Cristiano and Ramos during the celebrations.

Five minutes later, Marcelo drove a finish under Courtois and the result was sealed. 2-1.

But Cristiano still wanted his goal.

He picked the ball up on the left wing and skipped into the box, before Diego Godín tripped him over. Cristiano turned towards the ref to appeal for the penalty and, moments later, he was standing with the ball on the spot.

Cristiano strode forward and struck the ball hard to his right, watching the keeper dive the other way.

The ball rippled the back of the net. GOAL!

Cristiano ripped his shirt off and sprinted towards the fans, roaring as loudly as he could. He spotted his brother Hugo in the crowd and gave him a huge grin as he sprinted over to him.

"COME ON!" he shouted, punching the air. Real hadn't just beaten Atlético, they had thrashed them.

They had also done the one thing that Real Madrid teams had been attempting for years. They had achieved La Decima.

The next morning, there was a huge parade on the streets of Madrid, where thousands of fans came out to celebrate their team's tenth European trophy.

"What's next for us after La Decima then, Cris?" Carlo Ancelotti asked his star player.

"It's obvious isn't it, boss? We go for number eleven!"

17
DÉJÀ VU

May 2016, San Siro, Milan, Italy
Champions League Final, Real Madrid v Atlético Madrid

"Atlético will be out for revenge. We can't let them get a sniff," Real Madrid's new captain, Sergio Ramos, said, looking around at the players in the dressing room.

"Don't worry, we've got Cris," Karim Benzema replied. "This is his competition."

Cristiano smiled. It had been two years since La Decima, and in that time he had scored over 100 goals, including a personal record of 61, two seasons ago. He'd also won his third Ballon d'Or and become the top scorer in Real Madrid and Champions League history.

But, for all that, Real Madrid had failed to win any trophies. Meanwhile, Cristiano had had to watch Lionel Messi's Barcelona win two consecutive La Liga titles and the 2015 Champions League.

Carlo Ancelotti, the man who'd sealed La Decima, had left the club. Rafa Benítez had come and gone, and the new man at the helm was former Real Madrid legend, Zinedine Zidane.

He'd quickly gone about changing things within the team.

"It's easy to overthink tactics," he told the players in his first team meeting. We can try different formations and ideas, but at the end of the day we have incredibly good players here that can beat anyone, no matter what formation we play."

Zidane brought Brazilian defensive midfielder Casemiro into the team, to play behind Luka Modrić and Toni Kroos. Cristiano was given free reign on the left-hand side to cut in and get shots away.

The defence was marshalled by Sergio Ramos and Raphaël Varane, with Marcelo and Dani Carvajal as the full-backs.

Real were turning into one of the best sides in the world – without a single word of tactical advice.

They started a long way behind Barcelona in the league and, despite a 12-game winning run to end the season, they ended up finishing a point behind their rivals.

But Barcelona had faltered. They no longer had Pep, Xavi was gone and Iniesta was going. There were weaknesses in the Barca setup that Cristiano would be keen to exploit in the following season.

But today was the Champions League final, where once again Real faced Atlético Madrid.

And, as they sat in the dressing room, Cristiano's smile hid the fact that he knew he was carrying a knock and wasn't at 100% fitness. But there was no way he would miss this game – an opportunity to get his hands on a third Champions League title. Most people might only ever win one.

"We know how Atlético play," Zidane told his players.

"They sit deep, defend well and make it difficult. So Cris and Gareth, drift inside and find that gap between the full-backs and centre-backs. Let our full-backs occupy the wide positions."

Early in the first half, Gareth Bale flicked the ball on from a Toni Kroos free kick and Sergio Ramos poked it over the line, giving Real Madrid the lead.

Real controlled the remainder of the first half, but they couldn't find a second goal. At half-time, Atlético were the only side to make a change, bringing on the pacy Belgian winger Yannick Carrasco.

He made an instant impact, terrorising Dani Carvajal at right-back. Only a few minutes into the second half, Atlético won a penalty when Pepe clumsily fouled Fernando Torres, but Antoine Griezmann blasted the penalty against the crossbar.

"That's a warning!" Cristiano shouted. "We need to step it up now."

But Atlético continued to attack and Cristiano wasn't surprised when Yannick Carrasco equalised, blasting the ball into the net from a Juanfran cross.

Then, in stoppage time, Real Madrid won a corner.

The ball found its way to Cristiano, but he mistimed his jump and the ball hit his thigh and went wide.

"Come on!" he groaned, putting his head in his hands.

Years ago, at the beginning of his career, a miss like this would have left Cristiano distraught, devastated at losing the game for the team.

But experience had now caught up with him. He knew that, whatever happened on the pitch, he needed to refocus and get on with the game. This was business. There was no room for upset.

Two years ago, Real Madrid had scored three goals against Atlético during extra time, but this time neither team could find a breakthrough.

The final was going to be decided in a penalty shootout.

Cristiano had missed his penalty in the 2008 Champions League final with Man United, but he knew that wasn't going to happen this time.

"Let me go fifth," he said to Zidane.

"Are you sure?" Zidane asked. "We might need you earlier, to settle down some of the other lads."

"Trust me."

Eight penalties came and went before Cristiano stepped up. Seven of them were scored. It was Atlético and their right-back Juanfran who blinked first. His penalty struck the post.

Now, the pressure was on Cristiano. If he scored, Real Madrid would have European Cup number eleven. If he missed, the shootout would go on.

He took a deep breath, set himself, sprinted forward and blasted the ball to his right.

The world seemed to stop as Cristiano watched the ball fly towards the far corner. The keeper had gone the wrong way and, moments later, the ball was in the back of the net.

Real Madrid were Champions of Europe, once again.

Cristiano had scored the winning penalty in the Champions League final.

He knew it didn't get any better than that.

18

CHAMPIONS OF EUROPE

July 2016, Stade de France, Paris, France
European Championships Final, Portugal v France

"How did we make it this far?" Nani said to Cristiano. "We've only won once in 90 minutes. All the others have been shoot-outs and extra time."

Cristiano had been thinking the same thing. He wasn't sure how Portugal had made it to their second Euros final either. They'd drawn all of their group games, narrowly scraping through in third place after a

3-3 draw with Hungary. They'd beaten Croatia 1-0 in extra time, Poland in the quarter-finals after a penalty shootout, and Gareth Bale's Wales in the semis. Now they faced France, the tournament's hosts, looking to win their first trophy since Euro 2000.

"Well, all that matters now is the next 90 minutes, or 120," Pepe said. "However long it takes us to win."

"He's right," Cristiano said, standing up. "It doesn't matter how we got here," he said. "Not all of us played in 2004, against Greece, but most of us remember it. We were the hosts, the favourites," he continued. "And Greece dug in and outfought us. We had better players, but they worked hard and made it difficult."

He paused for a moment. "Today, we are Greece. They've got Pogba, Griezmann, Payet. They've got 70,000 fans cheering them on. They've had it easy to get here, but we've had to fight. We've got more desire. We will work harder than them, and we will win."

He looked around at the determined faces in front of him. France were favourites, but he really believed that Portugal could win this.

But that belief was shattered by Dimitri Payet after

just seven minutes. Not because he scored, or because he set up a goal, but because of a challenge. He clattered into Cristiano, who instantly felt his knee give way.

The physio told Cristiano the bad news. He should come off, especially if he wanted to avoid long-term damage. But Cristiano refused. Not so early on.

He fought on for another 20 minutes, battling against the pain in his leg, until he couldn't do it any more.

He slumped to the floor, feeling the tears welling up in his eyes. Not for the first time, he was leaving a European Championship final in tears.

He was taken off on a stretcher and replaced by Ricardo Quaresma. Cristiano could see the heads of his team-mates drop.

"The game's still going, lads," he shouted. "Let's stay focused. Keep up the pressure."

At half-time, Cristiano was even more involved. If he couldn't be out there on the pitch, he had to help from the sidelines.

"Guys, it's 0-0," he said. "They haven't scored, they haven't looked like scoring – and they're getting nervous. If we can find Nani and Ricardo, we can get openings.

They're not the quickest back there. Trust me, boys."

Cristiano spent the second half in the dressing room, being treated by the physio. The team fought hard, but after 90 minutes the game remained deadlocked.

There was still a chance.

"I'm going out there," Cristiano said, brushing the physio away. "They need me.'"

He limped out of the tunnel and approached the Portugal players, who were huddled around their manager.

"I'm so sorry, Cris ... " Ricardo Quaresma said.

"Don't worry about it," Cristiano interrupted. "Focus on the game. We've got 30 minutes to win our country's first trophy! Let's not lose this now. They're getting nervous – and the longer this goes on, the more they're going to panic. They will make mistakes."

Cristiano stood on the touchline during extra time, bellowing instructions, shouting at the defenders to close down, to get the ball to the strikers. He'd effectively become their manager.

Then, with 10 minutes left, a miracle happened. Eder moved into the middle, dragging the ball onto his right foot, and unleashed a low, driven shot. It whistled over the ground and flew into the bottom corner.

Portugal had the lead!

The next 10 minutes were some of the worst of Cristiano's life. Portugal fought and defended with everything they had – and Cristiano could only watch and hope that they held onto their lead.

He was shouting at the defenders, shouting at the referee, shouting at anyone who would listen. He needed this game to be over. He needed to win.

After an eternity, the final whistle came. Cristiano sunk to his knees, tears streaming down his face. He was crying again, but this time for a good reason.

Portugal were Champions of Europe. *He* was a champion of Europe once again.

After limping up the steps of the Stade de France to lift the trophy, Cristiano was walking back towards the pitch to celebrate with his team-mates and the Portuguese fans, when a familiar face approached him.

"You did good, son," Sir Alex Ferguson said, giving Cristiano a hug. "You did good."

19
CIAO

March 2019, Allianz Stadium, Turin, Italy
Juventus v Atlético Madrid

"Their players have got to be sick of the sight of you by now," Leonardo Bonucci said, glancing over at the Atlético Madrid squad, as he and Cristiano walked out onto the pitch.

"If they aren't already, they will be after today's game!" Cristiano laughed.

It had been two years since Bonucci and Cristiano had

lined up as opponents in the Champions League final. A year later, Real Madrid had won the competition for an incredible third year in a row, beating Liverpool 3-1 in the final. It was Cristiano's fifth Champions League, the most of any player in history.

But that match against Liverpool had turned out to be Cristiano's final game in a Real Madrid shirt. He hadn't planned on leaving Madrid, but he'd won everything there was to win in Spain and now he needed new challenges.

Cristiano didn't want just to be the best player in the world – he wanted to be the best in history. He wanted to try to win the Champions League with a new club.

So when Juventus paid 112 million euros to sign him, he became the most expensive player aged over 30 in history.

He could have gone anywhere in the world, but Juventus had been a club he'd admired for a long time. He'd watched them get so close to winning the Champions League, only to fall at the last hurdle to, of all clubs, Real Madrid. He knew he could take them one step further and lift the trophy.

That journey began tonight, against a familiar set of faces – Atlético Madrid.

Atlético had won the first leg 2-0 in Spain, and it was rare for a team to come back in the second leg from such a deficit. If Juventus were going to get through tonight, they would need a miracle.

Right from kick-off, the Atlético defenders didn't give Cristiano any space, marking him closely. They didn't want to let the man who'd caused them so much pain in the white of Real Madrid do it again for another club.

But 25 minutes in, he had his goal. A cross from Bernadeschi drifted towards the back post, where Cristiano was lurking. He rose high above the defender Juanfran to crash a header into the back of the net.

"That's one!" he roared. "Two more to go!"

And he was determined to get all of them.

A couple more times he went close in the first half, with powerful headers that were saved or drifted just wide.

"You've got them in the air, Cris," Mario Mandžukic′ said to him at half-time. "If we get the crosses in, you will score."

Cristiano nodded. He'd always been brilliant in the air and, as he'd got older, he'd found it harder to maintain the running and dribbling speed he used to have. But he still had his power in the air.

Early in the second half, João Cancelo dribbled down the right wing. A queue of Juventus players waited for the cross in the box, including Cristiano.

Once again, he soared above the Atlético defenders and met the ball with a powerful header.

But this time, the Atlético keeper Oblak was equal to it, clawing the ball away on the goal line. Cristiano chased down the rebound, but the ball was hoofed clear.

"Over the line!" Cristiano shouted to the ref.

There was a moment of silence as the Juve fans in the stadium held their breath. Then the referee pointed to the half-way line.

The goal was given.

"SIUUUUUU!" Cristiano roared, joining in with the fans in their celebrations.

Juventus were level on aggregate now. Another goal would take them through. And Atlético were stuttering. The nerves were getting to them.

For 40 minutes, Atlético held and held, looking to drag the game into extra time.

But then Bernadeschi skipped into the box, pursued by Ángel Correa. The Atlético player stuck out a leg, tripping Bernadeschi.

The ref had no choice. Penalty.

There was nobody else in the stadium who was going to take it – nobody else in the world who the Juventus fans would rather have standing over it. It was always going to be Cristiano.

He sprinted forward, blasting the ball hard to his left, watching as Jan Oblak went the other way.

The ball flew into the back of the net.

Cristiano had his three and Juventus had their three. Against the odds, they had beaten Atlético 3-2. They were going to the Champions League quarter-finals.

His time in Turin had just begun.

20
RECORD BREAKER

July 2020, Allianz Stadium, Turin, Italy
Juventus v Sampdoria

"Thirty goals is a great season, Cris," Paulo Dybala grinned.

"I'd be happy with 10 goals!" Blaise Matuidi laughed.

"I normally score 40 or 50," Cristiano shrugged. "But as long as we get our hands on the title tonight, it doesn't really matter."

"Nine in a row tonight, lads. That's the record!" Bonucci shouted.

"Then ten next year!" Cristiano replied. "Juve's version of La Decima!"

After beating Atlético, Juventus had been knocked out of the Champions League in the quarter-finals by a young and entertaining Ajax side. They won Serie A, but Cristiano finished the season with 28 goals, his lowest total since 2009.

In the summer, Cristiano had soon found his shooting boots again when he'd led Portugal to their second major trophy, winning the first Nations League tournament. He'd scored a hat-trick against Switzerland to reach the final, where Portugal had beaten the Netherlands 1–0.

The game had been held in Portugal, meaning that, as the team's captain, Cristiano had lifted the trophy in front of a home crowd in Porto. It was Cristiano's proudest moment in a Portugal shirt. He finally felt that he'd made up for losing to Greece in the final of Euro 2004.

Cristiano's family had also flown from Madeira to Porto to attend the game and watch Cristiano carry the weight of Portugal on his shoulders.

"I'm so proud of you, Cris," his mum told him after

the final. "Who'd have thought my baby boy would come this far from the streets of Funchal! Your father would be so proud of you."

Cristiano gave his mum a warm hug. His dad had died when Cristiano was just 20, but every day, Cristiano thought about how he wouldn't have even become a professional footballer if his dad hadn't become the kit man at Andorinha and convinced them to let his son play for them as a boy.

Tonight's match was against Sampdoria, and a win would seal Cristiano's second Serie A title with Juventus.

It would be strange winning the title in an empty stadium, but that was the nature of playing football during the pandemic. All that mattered was that they got the win, that they won the title.

But Sampdoria were solid, determined to hold out for as long as they could, to prevent Juve from winning the title tonight.

Just before half-time, Juventus got the goal. They won a free kick on the edge of the box and, instead of crossing it in, Pjanić cut it back to where Cristiano was lurking. He hit it hard, fizzing it past the keeper.

Juventus had one hand on their ninth consecutive league title and Cristiano had his 31st league goal of the season.

Juve continued to attack in the second half, desperate to get that second goal. Cristiano had a few efforts that were saved or blocked by the Sampdoria defence, and it was midway through the second half when one of these efforts was palmed in the direction of Bernadeschi, who tapped home.

"That'll do it, mate!" Cristiano said to Bernadeschi, as the players' celebrations echoed throughout the empty stadium.

Juve had their second goal and they had their title – their ninth in a row.

It was Cristiano's seventh league title over the course of his career, in three different countries.

Now they just needed to win the Champions League.

21
800 (AND ONE)

December 2021, Old Trafford, Manchester, England
Manchester United v Arsenal

"Lads, it's time to turn this around and charge into the top four." Cristiano looked around at the red shirts in the dressing room.

He was one of the senior players there, and it was to him that everyone was looking. He had to guide the rest of the team.

Cristiano had spent three seasons at Juventus. He'd

scored over 100 goals, won two Serie A titles and finished in his final year with the top goalscorer award.

But no Champions League. And now he was 36.

His time at Juventus was coming to an end. They were pushing for a younger team and had effectively told him he could leave.

He couldn't help but feel that he'd failed. He'd broken all sorts of records, but they'd not been the ones he'd wanted.

At his age, most players were winding down their careers. They would move to the MLS or to China, and enjoy one last big payday before they retired.

But that wasn't Cristiano's style. He still felt that he could play for years.

He'd had several offers from a number of clubs all over Europe, but there was one that drew his attention more than the others. Manchester United. The club where it had all begun.

He'd even had a personal phone call from Sir Alex Ferguson, imploring him to come back to Old Trafford.

It would be a genuine challenge, for sure. He would have to try to guide United back into the top four, back into the hunt for the Premier League title. It might turn out to be one of the biggest challenges of his career.

After a slow start to the season, United found themselves some way adrift of the top four. Ole Gunnar Solskjær was sacked and Ralf Rangnick was announced as the new manager.

"We win tonight against Arsenal and we close the gap to just three points from the top four," Cristiano told the players. "I know we've struggled this season, guys, but it's early. We can turn this all around. Trust me."

Cristiano had another reason to score tonight, too. A more personal reason. He was one goal away from reaching 800 career goals.

Most professional players never played 800 games, let alone scored 800 goals. Cristiano thought that scoring against one of United's biggest rivals would be the perfect way to reach the landmark.

There were many young faces in the United dressing room, including Jadon Sancho and Marcus Rashford. Cristiano thought back to when he was their age, looking up to the likes of Ryan Giggs and Roy Keane.

Now he was the guy the youngsters like Jadon and Marcus looked up to.

Arsenal took the lead early on when Emile Smith-Rowe fired home a bizarre opening goal, with David de Gea on the floor, injured.

It silenced the crowd for a while, and it wasn't until just before half-time that Man United levelled, when Bruno Fernandes smashed into the net.

Then, not long into the second half, the moment that Cristiano had been waiting for came. Marcus Rashford laid the ball back to him and he fired a shot into the net, sliding it past the Arsenal keeper.

It was his 800th career goal and, to make things sweeter, it was the goal to put United into the lead.

It only took a couple of moments for Arsenal to pull back level, with a goal from Martin Ødegaard.

Then, 15 minutes later, Ødegaard himself was involved again, this time taking out Fred in the box. After a quick VAR check, the referee pointed to the spot.

Penalty.

For the second time in the match, it was up to

Cristiano to put United ahead. If his 801st goal could secure the win for United, Cristiano wondered just how far The Red Devils could go under their new manager.

He took a deep breath, sizing up Ramsdale in the Arsenal goal. Then he charged forward and blasted it down the middle, as Ramsdale dived.

GOAL!

Cristiano was already wheeling away to celebrate.

It had been over 10 years since Cristiano had last played for United, and almost 20 years since he'd made his professional debut for Sporting Lisbon, but he was still delivering in the high pressure moments and scoring goals.

Whether it was La Decima, the Ballon d'Or or the Euros, Cristiano was never satisfied.

And, beyond all that, there was still one trophy that he hadn't won. The biggest of them all.

The World Cup.

At 36-years-old, Cristiano knew that Qatar 2022 would likely be his final chance to win that competition. But if he'd learnt anything in his glittering career, it wa that anything was possible.

After all, he was Cristiano Ronaldo, the greatest player in history – and he was still going.

HOW MANY
HAVE YOU READ?

 MESSI

 KANE

 RONALDO

 HAALAND

 SALAH

 PULISIC

 LEWANDOWSKI

 MAHREZ

 MBAPPÉ

 SON

 SAKA

 SANCHO

 FÉLIX

 GNABRY

 STERLING

 RASHFORD

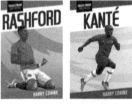 KANTÉ

 SILVA

 VAN DIJK

 SOUTHGATE

 GUARDIOLA